Dinner on the Lawn

Douglas Messerli

Sun & Moon Press

College Park, Maryland

ISBN: 0-940650-14-2

Grateful acknowlegment is made to the editors of the following journals and anthologies in which some of these poems first appeared: *Knock Knock: A Funny Anthology by Serious Writers, Là-bas, Roof,* and *Doc(k)s.*

Sun & Moon Contemporary Literature Series no. 7

Sun & Moon Press

4330 Hartwick Road
College Park, Maryland

"I am inclined to believe there is no
difference between clarity and confusion."

Gertrude Stein

for Howard

the initial process
to speak *in*
and even transcend
from a thinking
into
instances
too subtle to be
to be reflected to be
an obscurity
terrorizing the accent
of a word itself,
a...a cold finger,
toe, thigh against,
a kind of algebra
woven from what needs
to be hidden
between
knowledge
and effect—
this happens
or is an infatuation.
the seasons change.
I meet an old man.
it becomes the roof,
a small boat

a standing ''outside-the-ego,''
a pursuing of

that the word

to be convincing

has pretty much

to ignore

a simple emotional

(to say that

is never to be given—O

you there

on the beach!)

an act

equal to

relatively opaque

that invite

invites

the wood

to nail—

come up

to image

reconciliation

to "spring full-blown"

& sink

by thin

glimpse)

to enter

surface

to show

like glass

through

a pool of clear

a sky

or ledge

of cement

it is

& yet

is to know

to put,

viewed from

retreat,

to draw a symmetry

that crystals,

to reason this

like a geologist's contour,

as anyone

just knowing

singlemindedly

("Perhaps you should come upstairs..."

a worry

to graduate

a kind of fear,

to bow,

lean against the door

(to bungle

by interruption

seems *is* meoldramatic

in any *real*

taking) bewildered

of trying "I" am not

"someone else" in language,

to will

into credibility, even shape, mass
a daily feel of minuteness,
to be born into
not invisibly
a muscle-biting flesh
in a cerain year
month, day, hour

Ay Di Mi

to track—

                                       the quotidian

        of "machine   gasping coral,"

         "the sea & sepulchre"

         "the glassy country"

are words, encores   a summer sound,

       the lights even A...

                outer voice as ascertainable,

       bright. Corot is—ay di mi!

corrupting reverie

          it seeks

              intent aflame

Any & Every

Begin & begun.
As neglect
are frightened.
As pleases is precious
Rest.
At the door suddenly
a green weep.
No description. Or in fact
nearly frightened.
Living certainly uncertainly.
Poor dog. This is the story of
Naturally.
''Skull beneath skin.''
Are trees.
Full of sap.
Pale. His hands into water.
Here's—take it out!
Impersonal
(some say).
As puns dates of course are fruits.

Or history: 1980 12 o'clock.
If he does
make a note!
As accomodation for.
Houses have doors.
Particularly in Pittsburgh.

The Tides

sat on the very seat
    its black oak rooms
            overhead
   month's crop of hair hanging low
      (nothing human except salvage)
   that his facts come to him raw
         sometimes swept
  shipwrecked limp upon a platform
again when the current ran brisk
     pool where the dogs have brought otter
           to a stand
   without a voice
     swagger in the streets
    between sweet cakes, thin
       with deprecating smiles
  before the brown river water turns
pleasantly panted

        *

The shore: shells (clam, piss clam, oyster, mussel,
            barnacle, snail, lobster husk), seaweed
The body: sand (between the toes, in the knee bend,
            in the folds of the scrotum, in the button
            of the belly, in the arm pits), grit of
            the mouth
The birds: gulls, large gulls, pigeons, terns
The sky: overcast grey, a line of cobalt

                              *

            were pulling from
                        camera
      surface   stone
                              & fled to the southern coast
past steel & bone & muscle
                        patches of
                              brilliant sun
            I offer as self-defense
        the disappearing hills
                        lips of its bay
            so curved
                        you will always find shelter

                              *

South China

East China

North

Andaman

Yellow

Caribbean

Bearing

Baltic

Mediterranean

Red

Hudson Bay

Persian Gulf

Gulf of Mexico

Gulf of St. Lawrence

Sea of Okhotsk

Gulf of California

Sea of Japan

These are the seas,

Pacific

Atlantic

Indian

Arctic

the oceans

Overture

I a criminal
with what might be
unexpected,
that comes
outward
from an instinct
wringing
an empty
derived from
this to uncover
unfortunate luck
''as old as the hills''
neck & neck
(well, near it,
with renewed interest
given way
to familiarize
your breath
(death as the lawn
to cross)

shy
address & line
as words press
a coming into
flattery
for heroics,
quaking
from a further
indecision
to dwindle
to deny
the fold of

Look! even zero
is an open
these the spines
these the hidden:
''romance for breakfast
murder for lunch.''

Breakfast

not a few
wish for coffee
striking a bushel
of—scaredy-cat!
to wash a hand
into never-drunk water
or to clap
aground beans
& stand a ring for
Saturday or any Sunday
of the weak
daybreak of eggs
sometimes strong
sometimes but always
when an absolute
madness starts
disappearing quick
to bake a bread
or cut—smell the pan?
pinching up the Barcelona hot

Dinner on the Lawn

they use trained people behind graceful clumps
scattered tribes cleaning back on the lawn
(certainly it's there, not from friends
of this or those sorts
apparently central to the ultimate topiary
like ships pooling lengths they picked trimmed gardens,
stretch that the stands gather
order of herbaceous work
of ancient tree the trimmed resemble odd flowering
hedges. everything is peeping
examined standing fast there is & fixed between seams
clipped on custom, light —the ''damn affair—
pedestal acquaintances, but only locust
we 2 contain up form
his friends designing gardens, neighbors, himself
informal, he scarcely flowers. geometric back
bent small recognizable, each expects a corner-
central porch as if October is coming to them. the 3 of us
dark out until seen, birch paper
& neatness careful as Egypt. they're shaded in formal corners

are interferers of such windows tonight. their

gardens have driven a border, some of it inhabited completely behind

almost pleased lawns ordered to the carvings at the door

surprised & so close

In the Money

curl

to this voice

agh agh agh

that's it

a small hurt

blond on his heels

two deep in a bathtub

to live yes sir!

across or to use & never

lie sitting to win

our train into an open

press unembarrasment

to the blood

to yield

a gnaw

flowing or gulp

the bend to border

at every angle

to the brink of

up up up up up! completely
that's leaning
so there!
Ho Ha!
there'll be a hot
old love, a toast
to fight the snow
burly at the end
of twig

Solo

I fear
your eyes
to bruise
identity.
the thirst of
magnetism
carves itself
to matter—
ears, toes, head.
even now
a kneecap
bends
to decoy
an eyelash here.
the armpit
of unfamiliarity
under composure
smells, already spent
as unblush
familiar now

to express

by the knit

of brow

a hand on

or under

tokening

tokening

Nervousness

I walk down
what I've seen
out of sound
& always fear
burst in on us:
this morning
listening with you
going to bed
to get into
these sentinels
hands
missing the
in the chinks
or even prefer
above the wing
the false of his
asking
can you say if)
from wandering
''what good is it then?''

in the leaning
a wire to spread
falling into
not as speed
how if feels
but you & you

Solstice

you don't know
what adjustments
break out of
once having shaded against
coming into crystal
as dare. the sun
fat & white
too cold
to extend
to or express
takes it
straight unseen
to leaf
a slight!

Worm

not walled to beg, break
from upon a worn,
a horizontal, the gone
still as lower for the dark
oozing it through urgency
against a glisten, a cold hierarchy
facing to understanding
beats a vegetable to show
succulence, the slack
said to be continue
balancing a linger

Akimbo

over
a pot
    wrapped
        very
        tense
            to think
            of
            or smile
                at with
                    widowhood
                    such a
                    (delicate
                        fast-beating
                            out of
                                bed my sweet
                                    into
                                  a crater
                                      off
                                    her lap
                                        bring
                                      the fuss!

Leaving the House

for Howard

resembling

the cut

reserving

by the hang

beneath

the stale old

& older wet

the threadbare

content

stone by stone

to sever

or will

exhaust its object

through the door

to measure

now calm

a solitude

wanting

a hold

polar-white,
a soft
as arctic,
a lack
sequestered
to a tight
breathe then

far begin
to the almost
reach
I patch, compass
not the white
of our
but a gradual
"which shore?"
I sluggish
of curl
of plum

Visitation

for Larry Shifreen

out an angles

past indicative

to submit to

each other

split hairs

to get

that very next instant

a crop of

''weak

anger''

the shape of

crotchetiness

lizard-like

licking

those little green islands

up the trunk

over &

between

stone-

edged balance

to

on

just now

back into veins

slipping

in empty

a quiet motor *(naja naja*

that maps out

even before

faces

hit some current

or shape an inside

out of this

that divides

lucidity from

extinction

of a squeeze

black in crack

trying to repeat

"mercy"

or even taste

head-first

beneath

orientals

to explain

everything that *there*

is near

on the verge of

& under

Amelia Earhart

some credence

revives the pulse

it contains

to signal

the button

under shirt

to appear

like spots

of trouble's

unreadiness

to dive

as spread

in hoping

to take

the symptomatic

as it becomes

apparent

to expect

a repeat

against

where
I wear my shoulder
my heart

Encore

being what is
for a period
the blade
with some break
I
as chalk
on edge—
dirty white—
confess
inside to shreds
without

I must *be*
hunting
a blood of
on that gray
a somebody else
too remiss
for all their delusions.
the French

''by this sign
say thinking—
in each man's legend—
day to dark.
I'm not convinced.
even tomorrow
a fig must.

let us keep
to pull
a half-believing in
which to
we contort
the guts.

Palm

into the cut—now you *are*
polished to a round by what?
is it for the dead
limbs shore?
perhaps restlessness
lives afterward
still to be possessed
(hips to narrow to),
an apex of pursuit
pulling
out of sense
in detail
to furniture
the ''foot-in-the-grave''

Nostalgia

a white blown

to equal

the flash of nuts or snow

to calm

or tune a fork

over tongues

spring-naked

paper-thin

spokenness

of a salt to spin or

crack

cross-legged

before again

is put to

precipitate the old adamantcy

into fright

Space

for Charles Bernstein

O for O

the cheekbone

on fast feet

swore by

that would reach

to crown

or leaving

in & out

on the word

at some reprieve

of not being

the empty snarl

to find

into the waters

some port

without pitch

between tongues

to deal in

to pass

to return

that might turn

(dropping between

might know

(ten to one)

to the curb

as high

no matter what

Douglas Messerli was born in Waterloo, Iowa, and spent most of his childhood in the Midwest. He attended the University of Wisconsin and the University of Maryland, and he worked at Columbia University in New York before joining the faculty of Temple University, where he is currently Assistant Professor of English. His other books include *Some Distance* (1981) and *Djuna Barnes: A Bibliography*. Publisher and editor of *Sun & Moon: A Journal of Literature & Art* and Sun & Moon Press, he also has authored numerous essays on contemporary poetry and fiction. In 1981 he was awarded the CCLM (Coordinating Council of Literary Magazines) Fellowship for outstanding editing.